TOURING HEARTBEA[T]

This book is published by C.P. Printing and Publishing Ltd., on behalf of Ashley & Newey who own the sole rights to Heartbeat Holidays.

For further details of short breaks and touring holidays telephone (0325) 353839.

Ashley & Newey is a division of New World Hotels.

SPECIALIST CONSULTANTS
TO THE
HOTEL & CATERING
INDUSTRY

ASHLEY & NEWEY

P.O. Box 124,
Darlington, Co. Durham, DL2 2YX.

Heartbeat is a copyright trademark of

YORKSHIRE
TELEVISION

WELCOME TO 'HEARTBEAT' COUNTRY

Towards Westerdale

*"You can always tell a
Yorkshireman .... but not much!"*

Now, it is hardly surprising that this saying
is none too popular with us Yorkshire folk.
To those who have never visited our part of
the world, it would imply we are the sort of
people who think we're something special.
Well maybe we are, but *special* only in the
sense that we have the good fortune to live
in a very special place.

To those of us who were born in the county
of North Yorkshire, there is nowhere that
can compare with the breathtaking beauty
of the landscape. When you have the
splendour of the North York Moors National
Park literally on your doorstep, it is hard to
imagine anywhere more spectacular. Tucked
away in the far north-east corner of
Yorkshire, the Park is bounded on the east
by the precipitous coastline of the North
Yorkshire and Cleveland Heritage Coast. To
the west, the Cleveland and Hambleton
Hills form a steep escarpment with

dramatic views across to the Pennines while
to the south, in contrast, the land slopes
gently away towards the Vales of Pickering
and Mowbray.

The Park covers 553 square miles of rugged
upland which encompasses the largest
expanse of heather-clad moorland in
England. For many summer visitors, the
most memorable part of their trip is the
sight of the high moors in late July and
early August, a glorious sea of purple
heather intersected by soft green valleys or
dales. These are not the wide, majestic
rivers of the Yorkshire Dales, but shorter
streams which create landscapes of great
charm within a limited space: Farndale
with its famous daffodils, remote
Westerdale, steep-sided Newtondale and
Great Fryup Dale. Narrow roads snake
their way along the riggs or ridges between
these secluded dales and the unexpected
views are breathtaking. You can walk or
ride along almost 1,000 miles of paths and
bridle ways and discover a wilderness and

solitude rarely found in modern Britain, together with a fascinating network of ancient tracks, paved packhorse routes and Roman roads.

Man has always found a way of sustaining a living from the moors and happily progress has been slow to destroy the evidence of the past. The first people to inhabit the moors were 'hunters and gatherers' who appeared just after the last Ice Age some 10,000 years ago. Bronze Age tumuli and ancient standing stones still dot the moorlands in their hundreds; the Danes and Vikings who, despite their reputation for rape and pillage, also turned the City of York into a thriving commercial centre; the Romans used the moors as a military training area for their legions; ruined castles and abbeys recall past sieges and conflicts. Traditional villages centred around the church and green have retained their own unique charm, whilst market towns and sheep sales reflect a pattern of life that is slow to change.

Near Goathland

THE CONCEPT OF A NATIONAL PARK

To the visitor, it is important to understand the concept of the National Park. For a start, there are no clearly defined boundary walls or fences. It is an area of particular natural beauty sheltering flora and fauna which are either unique or very special to the area, which must be preserved as far as possible. Some of the land is managed by public bodies such as the Forestry Commission, but much is private property with strict rules governing building and development. The residents and landowners are also the custodians of this important piece of British heritage, and although there are few barriers to prevent tourists enjoying the scenery, it is worth remembering that a great deal of effort and care has gone into the preservation of the landscape we see today, to protect it for future generations to enjoy.

FOLLOW THE COUNTRY CODE

Visitors are encouraged not to leave litter and to be extremely careful when disposing of cigarettes, especially during the hot, dry summer months. The consequences of a moorland fire can be devastating, and it can take years for the area to recover. Throughout the region, over a thousand miles of public footpaths and bridle ways are clearly indicated by fingerposts and marked on Ordnance Survey Leisure Maps, together with many miles of green lanes and country roads: keep to these and there is no risk of trespassing. Avoid climbing over drystone walls; they take the farmers hours to repair! Dogs are welcome too, but remember worrying or even chasing sheep is a public offence and is a real danger to valuable animals.

THE MOORS & MONASTERIES

There is little wonder that for centuries the area was favoured by religious orders seeking a place of peace. St. Ailred, the third Abbot of Rievaulx Abbey in the 12th century, remarked on the tranquillity of the moors and dales:

> *"Everywhere peace, everywhere serenity and a marvellous freedom from the tumult of the world."*

The moors boast some of the finest examples of religious architecture in the land. Sadly, many of the great monastic houses are now nothing more than ruins, ravaged by invaders from the north and stripped of their treasures by Henry VIII during the Dissolution of the Monasteries. Yet they still retain some of their original splendour, with their grand facades, peaceful gardens and landscaped grounds. From the high headland of Whitby, where the haunting ruins of the town's 13th century Abbey look out over the harbour, to Gisborough Priory, Mount Grace Priory near Osmotherley and many more sites in between, the moors have been a place of refuge and contemplation for centuries. The famous Synod of Whitby met at Whitby Abbey in A.D. 664 to adopt the Roman, rather than the Celtic, method of dating Easter, so bringing together the Irish and southern monastic communities under a common authority.

Monasteries became some of the richest landowners in the area, so it is hardly surprising that, freed from the power of the Pope, Henry VIII went on to destroy them to replenish the treasury coffers! By March 1540 the monasteries were no more. Their roofs stripped of lead, they fell into ruin, a useful source of building materials for the cottages and farms of nearby villages. Many have gone forever or, like Rosedale Abbey, can only be located by a few piles of stones. Yet the peace and tranquillity of these places can still be enjoyed as they were centuries ago by the monks of the time.

Today, eight centuries later, little has changed: peace and serenity still reign supreme on the wide expanse of the moors and the cosy, welcoming shelter of the dales. The pace of life has quickened a little, but in the way a grandfather clock would gain a minute or two every few months.

Whitby Abbey

TIME TO ENJOY . . . . .

Time is a very precious commodity to all of us, and on the moors every minute seems to last much longer. The narrow, twisting lanes force you to drive more slowly than on one of the characterless, monotonous motorways. When was the last time that you actually enjoyed a drive down a motorway? Heading along the moor roads, through tiny villages and sheltered dales, gives you the chance to see the countryside and actually enjoy it. Turning a corner here is an adventure; there could be a picturesque village, or a vast expanse of purple moor over the next hill, or a glimpse of one of the lovingly restored steam trains from the North York Moors Railway in the valley below.

The pace of life here is slow and fulfilling; nobody rushes, everything gets done in its own allotted time. Life is governed by the seasons: lambs are born in the spring, crops grow and ripen in the summer, and in the autumn, the land is prepared for sowing. Even the winter is a time for repairs and renewal, a time for reflection and planning for the year ahead.

THE PEOPLE AND THEIR CULTURE

Despite the staggering beauty of the place, the North York Moors is a tough and uncompromising environment in which to live. It is almost as if the moors are making a 'bargain' with those who settle here: if you can learn to live with the harsh, bleak winters and respect the laws of nature, you are rewarded with the beauty of the landscape and the breathtaking colours of the changing seasons.

The people of the moors have developed a way of life which is inextricably linked with the economy of the area, and they have a culture which is unique. There is a strong sense of community, where farmer, fisherman, shop-keeper and craftsman all work towards maintaining this special place. Every village has its own social structure, folklore and local celebrations which have been built up over centuries.

The people are hardy and friendly and their dry humour is, at first, almost incomprehensible to 'incomers' (the local term for visitors or people who have moved to the area, or anyone who wasn't born here). The moorfolk are open and direct, they have no time for "messing on with daft talk", but given time even the most cynical 'incomer' is won over by their warmth and good humour.

LITERARY INSPIRATION

With all this breathtaking scenery and unique culture around there is little wonder that the region has inspired people to write, the Brontës being perhaps the most famous of those who found inspiration on their travels through the region. The book that brought the moors in all their awesome glory to the world has to be "Wuthering Heights", a powerful and stormy love affair between Heathcliff and Kathy set amongst the equally powerful and stormy landscape of the Ilkley and North York Moors.

In later years, the experiences of a country vet in and around the moors were to be the inspiration for James Herriot's "All Creatures Great and Small" which eventually found huge success as a television series.

The moors have also inspired another local author to write about his experiences — the experiences of a village policeman. Peter Walker started to record his rich and varied life as a young constable in the 1960's on the moors beat. Recently retired as an Inspector, after serving 30 years with the North Yorkshire Constabulary, to concentrate on his writing, Peter Walker is author of some 70 books. Many are crime fiction novels written under pen names as well as "Folk Tales from the North York Moors" and "Murders and Mysteries from the North York Moors"; under the pseudonym of Nicholas Rhea he has published "Portrait of the North York Moors" and the "Constable" series, the first being "Constable on the Hill" (1979) and the 12th, "Constable by the Stream" (1991). As James Ferguson he is author of several "Emmerdale" novels based on the highly successful Yorkshire Television series "Emmerdale Farm", and has written three non-fiction titles about the area: "The Emmerdale Farm Book of Country Lore", the "Emmerdale Farm Official Companion" and "Emmerdale's Yorkshire".

Peter Walker is a prolific writer and contributes articles on rural matters and all aspects of country life to several newspapers and publications in the area. He has now settled comfortably in Ampleforth with his wife and four children to enjoy a very successful second career.

Ralph Cross, emblem of the North York Moors National Park.

HEARTBEAT – THE SERIES

Goathland

The HEARTBEAT stories are a superb adaptation by Yorkshire Television of the original 'Constable' books set against the backdrop of the North York Moors. They feature the principal character of P.C. Nick Rowan (played by Nick Berry) and his wife Kate (played by Niamh Cusack), superbly supported by Bill Maynard (of 'Selwyn Froggit' and 'The Gaffer' fame) as Claude Jeremiah Greengrass, the local ne'er-do-well and Derek Fowlds (the long-suffering Permanent Private Secretary in 'Yes Minister' and 'Yes Prime Minister') as Sgt. Blaketon.

The series draws on the wonderful characters from the 'Constable' books, and highlights the sense of humour of the moor folk, as well as showing the harshness and drama of life in the moors in the 1960's. The series is filmed in and around the picturesque village of Goathland (Aidensfield) as this is one of the many areas that has hardly changed over the years. Set on the main line of the North York Moors Steam Railway, the village boasts a delightful little station, and the trains feature frequently in the episodes.

TALKING TO THE CAST OF HEARTBEAT

During a welcome break in their busy schedule, I was able to talk to some of the main characters about the series. Without exception they all enjoyed being on location in such a beautiful part of the country, and were delighted by the warmth and hospitality of the local people.

BILL MAYNARD
alias Claude Jeremiah Greengrass

Bill Maynard breezes through the village dressed in character, as always, in a huge ex-World War II army greatcoat, a genial giant of a man with the unkempt appearance of a well-fed tramp.

"This is the most enjoyable job I have ever had, it's like being on holiday. I walk about with a permanent smile on my face".

Bill was settled comfortably in an armchair in front of a blazing fire in the lounge of

'The Inn on the Moor' in Goathland, referred to as "Base Camp" by the cast and crew during location shooting. During his long career in show business (he started at the age of 8), Bill Maynard has been a Butlins Red Coat, a stand-up comedian, had his own television series in the 50's and 60's, developed the characters of Selwyn Froggit and The Gaffer in sitcoms in the 70's and . . .

"Filled in my spare time with a bit of serious acting in the theatre doing Shakespeare and modern drama".

When Bill was discussing the character of 'Greengrass' with the author, Peter Walker, it turns out that the original 'Greengrass' was a "skinny ferret of a man".

"As I am six foot one and a 'trim' 20 stone, I had to fill the character out a bit."

By this time, Bill was in full flow, delighted to be given the opportunity to talk about the series and how much he was enjoying being part of it. The costume which he wears for the character is made up of varying bits and pieces from his other characters. The old suit is one which he wore in 'The Gaffer'; the shirt was from 'Selwyn Froggit' and the boots, well they have a history all of their own. Proudly displaying the huge, now brown, boots, he told me that they had originally been given to him brand new for the shooting of "Adolf Hitler, My Part In His Downfall" (Bill played a Sergeant in the film), based on the wartime adventures of Spike Milligan.

"Whenever we used to do any army film, we were always issued with new boots. By the time you'd broken them in, after about three to four weeks, the shooting was over".

The boots, shiny and new and their original black colour, were, according to Bill, probably Canadian Army issue.

"They were so soft and comfortable, they

couldn't have been British Army issue, they fitted like a pair of slippers from the first day so I kept 'em. I wore them all through Selwyn and The Gaffer, and a stage tour of 'Hobson's Choice', and somewhere along the way we had to change the colour to brown".

The boots, still brown and looking every bit as scruffy as Bill, are still giving good service in 'Heartbeat'. In developing the character of 'Greengrass' Bill decided to add the 'twitchy eyes'.

"I got that idea from an old rascal I knew once. He would always screw up his eyes and twitch when he told lies, and as the character I'm playing is a devious old villain, I 'twitch' my eyes whenever I'm supposed to be lying or embarrassed".

Bill reckons that 'Heartbeat' has become a success because of the variety, as well as having a . . .

"Damn good story line; there are aspects of 'Dixon of Dock Green' and 'All Creatures Great and Small' as well as the nostalgia of the music from the era which is brilliantly woven into the story".

Just as Bill was getting his second wind, a young production assistant arrived to take him off for his next scene.

"I ask you, is this any way to treat a pensioner?" said Bill with a cheeky grin and 'twitching' eyes, as he shuffled off like a khaki-covered mountain.

NIAMH CUSACK
alias Kate Rowan

The part of Kate Rowan, P.C. Rowan's wife, is played by Niamh (pronounced "Niev") Cusack. Niamh is the talented daughter of one of Ireland's most noted actors, Cyril Cusack. She was brought up in Ireland and started her stage career in Dublin. Although most of her career to date has been in the theatre, even working with her father and two older sisters in a stage production of "Three Sisters" by Chekhov, Niamh has been in a few films. This was her first venture into television and

working on a series set in the heart of North Yorkshire was a revelation to her. We managed to snatch a few moments of Niamh's time as she was between scenes.

"Having spent most of my time in England in and around London, I used to think that England only consisted of big cities, so being up here in this beautiful countryside is a revelation. I love open spaces and wild countryside — this is perfect — and I especially love it in the winter months".

Niamh's character, Kate, is usually seen on the move, portraying a busy country doctor. I asked her how she spent her time during breaks in the shooting.

"I love to go for long walks over the moors. Here you can go for miles and not see another living soul other than the sheep. It's also a place where I read much more, and catch up with letters that I have to answer. You have so much more time which you don't have in the city, and that's in spite of the fact that we have a very busy schedule".

Despite the busy schedule, Niamh was

looking relaxed and thoroughly enjoying talking about the series.

"I would seriously think about living up here if I knew that I would be working more in Yorkshire. It's a much better way of life and the people are great, they are earthier and not what I imagined. My impression of English people before I came up here was that they were quite private, very reserved. People here are not at all reserved; they are direct, they tell you exactly what they think, and it doesn't matter if you are a "Heartbeat" actor or one of the locals, that's one of the many things that I love about this place".

Because the cast and crew spend long hours in each others company, I asked Niamh how they all get on with each other.

"Well, we have to get on with each other — if we didn't it wouldn't work. Everyone is very friendly and helpful towards each other — that's part of the 'genius' of casting a group of people who are going to have to work closely together for six or seven months. It's not just a matter of whether they can act or not, it's also about whether they have the personalities which can complement each other. No one can be a 'prima donna' here, there isn't the time for that, and we give each other 'space' . . . it's not so friendly that you cannot breath".

The series seems to have captured the 'community' feeling which Peter Walker so successfully put across in his books, and the cast seem to have worked especially hard to fit in with the people around them.

"There is a wonderful community spirit about the stories. Up here, I think they have been blessed in that the locals are so game. We're now on our second series and some of the locals are as 'pro' as we are, some of them more 'pro' than I am. They know the camera angles, when they're out of shot, they really enjoy it and it's they who give it a sense of authenticity. I'm glad that we came a little earlier this time, the autumn colours of the moors are spectacular, the place is so beautiful."

I was intrigued to know how Niamh found

working with Nick Berry, her screen husband. They always appeared to be comfortable with each other as husband and wife on the screen, so how did they get along off-screen?

"Nick's great, he has a very gentle nature and he is easy to work with".

I mentioned that during the day we had always seen him looking very serious. Niamh laughed and told me . . . .

"He is probably thinking about the football results; he absolutely loves the game and follows the results wherever we are. I think that if Nick was ever asked to manage a football club, he would give up acting and do it like a shot. We hardly ever see him between shots because he's always reading through a huge pile of football magazines."

Sadly, Niamh had to rush off for another costume change for her next scene, but she certainly hopes that 'Heartbeat' will run for several more series so that she can return to this lovely part of the country.

NICK BERRY
alias P.C. Nick Rowan

The first snow of the year was coming down with a vengeance, mixed with freezing rain and a biting wind. The location was the gate to 'Upper Gill Farm' (Hunt House farm just outside Goathland), where the camera crew from Yorkshire Television were filming a sequence for an episode in series 2 of HEARTBEAT. It was 9 a.m. and the cast and crew had been on location since 7.15 a.m. The place was a hive of frantic activity, despite the awful weather, as cameras were repositioned, lights adjusted and microphones and sound cables put into place. The activity was centred around a single character stood by the farm gate, clad head to toe in souwester, huge black oilskins and wellingtons. This was Nick Berry, alias P.C. Nick Rowan on duty outside 'Upper Gill Farm' — scene of a suspected outbreak of foot and mouth disease. The scene was made even more bizarre by the collection of brightly coloured golf umbrellas that came out in between shots in a vain effort to keep the cast dry! Not even the fickle British weather could stop the production schedule though; every day of shooting has to produce 10 minutes of the episode no matter what, and 5 days of shooting equals a whole episode of 50 minutes for transmission. Despite the freezing conditions, the production team worked like a well-oiled machine with only the very worst of showers, and the occasional low flying RAF jet trainer, bringing things to a halt. Nick, ever the calm professional, took it all in his stride, displaying a quiet calmness and his almost permanent cheeky grin.

At the end of a hard and extremely cold day, I spoke to Nick who was thawing himself out in front of the fire in the lounge of the 'Inn on the Moor'.

Nick had been to Yorkshire before, but only on tour to places such as Leeds and Sheffield and had never seen the countryside.

"During the filming of the first series, we started doing some of the scenes at our other location just outside Otley. It was very pretty in Otley, but they said wait till you see Goathland. That first drive in across the moors, off the A64 through to Pickering, was absolutely stunning. Since filming around here, I have had time to explore it a lot more, and it's a really good

place to be. I brought my family up here last Easter and showed them around; they really loved it up here".

As the shooting of the series went on for approximately 20 weeks, and everyone worked and lived so closely, I asked Nick how he got on with the rest of the cast.

"They're a lovely bunch to work with, they keep it all alive and happy. During the winter months when it gets very cold, people tend to get bad tempered and irritable — but not with this group. We always find something to laugh about".

Having watched Nick working for two days it came across that he worked very hard at getting the character right and I asked him if he was conscious of the effort that he put into portraying P.C. Rowan.

"I wasn't aware of it, but I think it is very important that the character I'm playing is believable, but actors have different ways of working at the characters they play".

In the series, P.C. Rowan is an 'outsider' to the area. What did he think about that aspect of the character?

"Storywise there is more conflict than in the actual book and from a dramatic point of view, there is much more scope for the series and the characters. It highlights the north-south divide which I should imagine was even stronger 30 years ago when these stories take place.

The local people have been great; they are friendly and very accommodating and have told us that they really enjoy having us here. In London, nobody has any time for you, they are in a constant rush, so here it is so nice to be able to just sit down and relax. At night, especially, you can hear absolutely nothing. I couldn't get used to it, I couldn't sleep at first. I'm so used to hearing sirens wailing, traffic in the street, glasses smashing and people shouting, but that's the way I have always lived, being a 'city boy'."

I asked about his passion for football.

"It is something that has kept me going during the breaks in shooting. I was invited to take part in a programme for Radio 5 called "Fantasy Football" — there's about a dozen of us, people like Tommy Docherty and other players and managers who have a fantasy £10 million to spend at the beginning of the season to buy players for their team. If one of your players scores a goal during a match you gain points, but if they concede a goal you lose points. It's great fun and I find it a good way to relax at the end of the day. I'm a football 'maniac' — it's becoming a bit obsessive — but it eases the pressures that get to you in this business. Because of the success of the series, I've become involved with a lot of music recording, and it takes up a lot of my weekends off. If I'm not here then I'm usually in the recording studios".

We talked about the future of the series, and how Nick felt about being involved in a further series.

"I hope it carries on for a long time. I love doing it and I hope that they can keep coming up with good story lines for the scripts. It also seems to have been good for the tourism industry up here. Because it's so beautiful, people want to come and see it for themselves."

Finally, I asked Nick if there was anything about making the series that he *didn't* like.

"Early mornings", he said without hesitation. "I've never got used to getting up early. I find that part very difficult, I do miss my sleep".

After the long hard day we had both had, it seemed a good idea to let him go and get a well-earned rest.

DEREK FOWLDS
alias Sgt. Blaketon

In the confines of his "dressing room", (in reality a tiny caravan tucked away behind the fleet of production vehicles on the car park of the Inn on the Moor) Derek was thawing out after a scene at the farm gate location. He is probably best remembered for being 'Mr Derek' in a double act with 'Basil Brush', (the partnership was to last 5 very happy years.) He later appeared as the long-suffering, and at times totally confusing, Bernard the Permanent Private Secretary to the Minister in 'Yes Minister' and then 'Yes Prime Minister', both programmes hugely successful. But Derek had always been seen as a comedy actor.

"This is the first drama series that I have been a regular in. I've often been a regular in comedy series, and this is very different for me. It's great to be involved with this lot".

I asked Derek what he thought of the character he was playing.

"Well, first of all I'm a southerner, so to play a Yorkshireman was a terrific challenge, and also he's quite an extrovert. He's a strange one is Oscar Blaketon and I thought that this was an opportunity to do something I've never done before, to go out and take a few risks. As the series goes on, I hope to develop the character. I would like to be able to 'peel back' some of the layers to Oscar, to let people see what is behind the uniform and the sergeant's stripes, and to show why he behaves the way he does".

So, what has been the reaction to a southerner playing a Yorkshireman, especially here in the depths of the North York Moors?

"I was very worried to say the least, but the people up here have been absolutely fantastic. Coming back up here to Goathland to do the second series is almost like coming home, they look after us wonderfully. I have not had one criticism of my accent from any of the local people, and I take that as a great compliment".

Like all the other people I had talked to during my visits to the locations, Derek looked very happy and relaxed.

"It's easy to relax and enjoy what you're doing if you're working with professionals, and this crew, who are nearly all the same people from the first series, are a joy to work with. There's a great camaraderie amongst this lot; they work such long and very strange hours but they loved doing the first series and were very excited to be doing this one. Its great coming to work".

What did he think was responsible for the enormous success of the first series?

"Four things really. The location is perfect; the period is right because there are now so many people in their mid forties who grew up in that era, its great nostalgia for them; the music of the time was also great and it's used very well throughout the episodes; and lastly the scripts. We've had some cracking scripts to work with, the stories and the characters have been excellent. Plus we have had some really good actors making guest appearances each week as new characters, people such as Peter Barkworth, James Hazeldene from 'London's Burning', Rachel Davis from 'Making Out' — it all helps to keep the thing fresh and alive. We were all very much surprised that the first series reached a peak of fourteen and a half million viewers first time out".

The original characters of 'Greengrass' and 'Blaketon' were totally different in the books; Blaketon was the big, burly man and Greengrass the small, shifty one. When Derek was called to discuss the part he was quite surprised at being offered Blaketon.

"I nearly talked myself out of a job! I thought that Bill was the right person for the Sarge, not me. But I think that we have managed between us to get the balance and the 'friction' between them right".

The weather outside had taken a turn for the worse, though Derek and I couldn't decide if we could hear thunder, or our stomachs rumbling. So, as it was so near lunch time, and a wonderful aroma of roast pork was drifting from the kitchen, I asked Derek what he would remember most about his time up here.

"The best thing I have had said to me on this series, and it has happened on three occasions, once in Otley and twice up here, is 'Who do you base your character on because we have a Sergeant exactly like Blaketon!' I take that as a great compliment that I have made him so believable".

With that, we both made a dash through the rain to the roast pork!

PUTTING IT ALL TOGETHER

The logistics of making 13 episodes of what is now a major ITV series are mind-blowing. Every little detail has to be planned with the precision of a military operation, every eventuality has to be allowed for. Furniture which was current in the period has to be found, vehicles which are now 30 years old have to be located and transported to the middle of the moors, and that alone poses the problem of where they are to be parked and looked after as well as the fleet of huge trucks containing everything from cameras and generators to props and costumes.

Vehicles, by comparison to people, are an easy problem to deal with; ensuring the comfort and well-being of a hard-working cast and production crew is essential if the whole project is to succeed.

There is nothing glamorous about working in television, especially when the crew have to film a sequence on a bleak, cold, windswept moorside in the pouring rain. It only appears glamorous when we are watching the finished result from the comfort of our living rooms. On such a day, the catering truck is one of the most essential vehicles on the location, providing everyone with hot meals and a never-ending supply of tea, coffee and biscuits, the 'life savers'.

This important task had fallen to the firm of GT Caterers of Leeds who specialise in providing a total catering service for film and television locations. In the deliciously aromatic warmth of the catering truck — a huge beast with a fully equipped kitchen — the job of feeding a cold and hungry crew was under the control of Steve and John plus their hard-working crew. Steve has travelled the U.K. and Europe on some very exotic locations.

"We recently had to take the whole lot down to Athens. It took us four days of hard driving, which wasn't helped when the brand new engine in the dining bus blew up on us in the middle of France. But we made it on time, only just though".

As Steve chatted, he heaved a huge sizzling joint of pork out of the oven.

"We worked on the first series of "The Darling Buds of May" down in Kent, and we prepared all the food that is seen in the opening title sequence and for all the other scenes during the series", he said with justifiable pride. Steve and his team had also just finished working on a new series with David Jason called "A Touch of Frost" which will be coming to the screens very soon.

"The most important thing in this business is to always be one step ahead, especially when the shooting is on a very tight schedule. Whatever we serve is always greatly appreciated, and there are rarely any left-overs. Also, we only use fresh

ingredients. All the vegetables, meat, poultry and fish are bought locally which is most important, because then I know the people who supply us and I can be sure that everything is really fresh".

I can testify to the excellence of the soup which was most welcome after standing around on the farm location that morning in the driving rain. Steve had a wonderful recipe for 'spicy meatballs' which deserves a place in culinary history, along with the sausage rolls, fruit scones and eccles cakes, all freshly baked that day.

The crew (which consists of up to 50 people) and cast work to a very precise schedule for anything up to 20 weeks, and even the slightest hiccup could bring a whole day's shooting to a grinding, and very expensive, halt. But somehow it all comes together to bring the 'magic' of television drama to our screens for one hour every week for thirteen weeks; during which the next series is being planned and organised.

TOURING
HEARTBEAT
COUNTRY

STOCKTON-ON-TEES

MIDDLESBROUGH

GUISE

A1085

A66

DARLINGTON

A67

Hemlington

Nunthorpe

A172

New

A66(M)

BLACKWELL

CROFT-ON-TEES

A1(M)

A167

A67

B1264

GREAT AYTON

STOKESLEY

Crathorne

Easby

Great Smeaton

A19

A172

Carlton

Great Brot

Cringle Moor

CLEVELAND HILL

Swainby

Sheepwash

Cleveland Tontine

Chop

B1257

A167

Osmotherley

Snilesworth Moor

A684

Brompton

NORTHALLERTON

HAMBLETON HILLS

Nether Silton

BILSDALE

H

A168

Hawnby

Old Byland

Cold Kirby

Scawton

THIRSK

A170

Sutton-under-Whitestonecliffe

Oldstead

Wass

Kilburn

Coxwold

Redcar

Saltburn

B1269
A173
H
A174

Loftus
Boulby
Staithes

Hinderwell
Runswick
Kettleness

A171
A174
Sandsend

rry Topping
A171
Lythe
A174

Scaling Dam
Ugthorpe
WHITBY

Commondale

KILDALE
Danby
Lealholm
A171
SLEIGHTS
Hawsker

Castleton
Esk Valley Line
Egton
GROSMONT
ROBIN HOOD'S BAY

eenhow
ESKDALE
Glaisdale
B1416

WESTERDALE
Egton Bridge

Beck
Hole
Ravenscar

Westerdale Moor
Egton High Moor
GOATHLAND
A169

ROSEDALE
Goathland Moor
Fylingdales Moor
A171

Church Houses
Wheeldale Moor
Lilla Cross

FARNDALE
Rosedale Abbey
Harwood Dale

Low Mill
BRANSDALE
Blakey Ridge
Saltergate
North York Moors Railway

Spaunton Moor
Silpho

Hutton-le-Hole
Stape
NEWTONDALE
Hole of
Horcum
Langdale End
Hackness

Gillamoor
Langdale End

Lastingham
Newton-on-Rawcliffe
Levisham
FORGE VALLEY

Spaunton
Cropton
Lockton
TROUTSDALE
SCARBOROUGH

Fadmoor
Appleton-le-Moors
Low Dalby

Carlton
Beadlam
Sinnington

1257
KIRKBYMOORSIDE
Aislaby
A169
Ayton

HELMSLEY
A170
PICKERING
Thornton Dale
A170

Snainton

Oswaldkirk
th

FITTING IN WITH THE LOCALS

Making the series is hard enough, but without the co-operation and support from the residents in and around Goathland, it would be nigh on impossible. Fortunately the locals have taken 'HEARTBEAT' to their "hearts" and look on it as something of a community project. Many of the residents can be seen as extras in the episodes, and one of the cast actually commented that some of them are as accomplished as professional actors and a pleasure to work with.

North Yorkshire Police as officers are drafted in from local stations to keep the traffic moving around the action. It can be a bit confusing when the pub car park is suddenly teaming with policemen, some real and some from the series!

Everyone in the village feels that they have some small part to play in helping bring the series to life, even if it is just putting up with the disruption of their otherwise quiet and peaceful way of life for a few weeks every year.

There are, however, several benefits. The series has created a boost for the local economy, earning revenue for the local people employed on the series. Everyone connected with Yorkshire Television has a commitment to supporting the local tradespeople, purchasing their supplies and accommodation within the village as much as possible, as well as attracting tourists to this beautiful area — or 'Heartbeaters' as they have become known to the locals.

The transformation of Goathland into 'Aidensfield' requires a huge community effort on behalf of the local residents; they regularly find the local pub has been renamed, the yellow lines outside the houses have, temporarily at least, been painted over, and the local garage has extended its services to include "funeral directors" as well as serving petrol. Traffic through the village has to be halted during shooting which needs the willing co-operation of the real

HEARTBEAT DRIVES

Anyone who is a devotee of the "Constable" books and "Heartbeat" series can have a great time on these drives trying to fit the real places to the fictional place names that are used by the author. As the characters in the books are based on real people and the events that affected their lives, it is only natural that Peter Walker would invent new names for the locations in order to respect their confidence. Part of the fun of writing this book was to try and piece together this 'jigsaw puzzle' of places on the map. Several places referred to actually do exist: Middlesbrough, Northallerton, Malton, Thirsk and Scarborough. The fictional ones were not so easy to find! *"Aidensfield"* where P.C. Rowan lived and worked is Goathland; *"Eltering"* could be Pickering and *"Strensford",* mainly because it is a seaside town, could well be Whitby. As for the rest, well, your guess is as good as mine. Have fun, and even if you don't succeed in your detective work you will certainly enjoy the beauty of "HEARTBEAT COUNTRY".

DRIVE 1 — (67 miles)
THE CENTRAL DALES AND ESK VALLEY

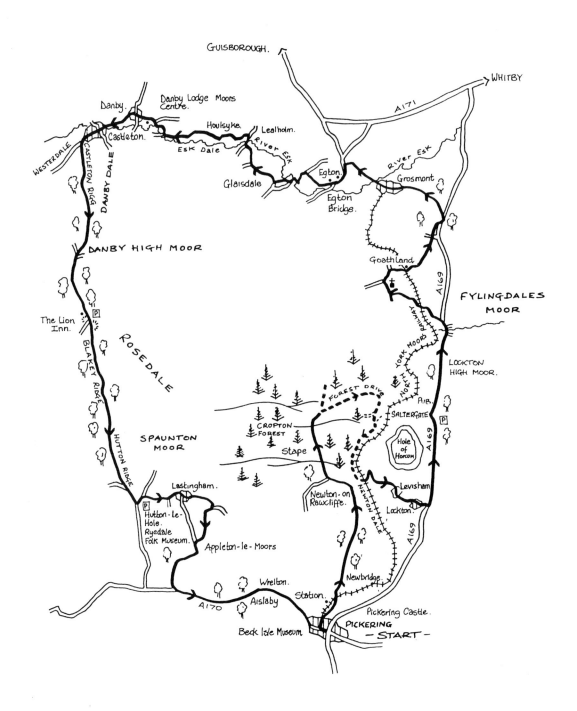

The busy market town of **Pickering** (*"Eltering"?*) with its ruined castle and fine 15th century church is the starting point for this entertaining drive over high moorland, with superb views over green dales and picturesque villages. From the town centre, follow signs for the North York Moors Railway and Besk Isle Museum. You will find a car park on the left just past the station buildings, the southern terminus of **The North York Moors Railway.** If you want to see the moors from a most unique viewpoint it is well worth taking a trip on one of the beautifully restored steam trains for a nostalgic 18-mile ride along the route of George Stephenson's original line, built in 1836.

The North York Moors Railway

Turn left out of the car park and drive on towards Newton-on-Rawcliffe. Look out for the **Moorland Trout Farm** on the left where you can buy fresh fish from the farm shop or feed the trout. Drive on over Newbridge junction into **Newton-on-Rawcliffe,** an attractive little village set around a central green, complete with pond and ducks! Drive on through the village and bear right where the road forks. Continue for 1½ miles to **Stape** and on into the **North Riding Forest Park,** the road giving way to an unsurfaced lane. Where the lane forks, bear right and drive on through **Cropton Forest** towards Levisham station, where a small toll is payable. Keep to the main track and avoid any side lanes. Eventually the track bears right round a tight bend to run parallel to the North York Moors railway down to the left along **Newtondale.** This narrow, steep-sided valley slices through the very heart of the

moors, carved out by the meltwater which came off the moors towards the end of the Ice Age. The variety of scenery along its length, the moorland, forest thickets and crags, support a wide range of animals and plants, which led to part of it being designated a Site of Special Scientific Interest. Drive over the crossing at Levisham station and follow the narrow lane which zig-zags up the far side of the dale to **Levisham** village. If the weather is fine, sit outside the Horseshoe Inn at the top of the main street and contemplate the delights of this sleepy, one-street village with its spacious grass verges, old cottages and farms. Suitably refreshed, head out of the village through **Lockton** to the A169 and turn left towards Whitby. After 2 miles, stop in the large parking area on the right and cross the road to look at the **Hole of Horcum,** a huge natural amphitheatre which, according to legend, was scooped out of Levisham Moor by the giant Wade.

Fylingdales Early Warning Station

Follow the A169 past the legendary Saltergate Inn over **Fylingdales Moor.** Over to the right, the 3 huge white protective domes of the Ballistic Missile Early Warning System resemble giant golf balls visible for miles around. As the road drops down over a small stone bridge at Ellerbeck, take the left turn on the far side for **Goathland** and Beck Hole. Cross Goathland Moor before descending into the village past the Mallyan Spout Hotel and drive along the wide common shorn smooth by wandering sheep. You are now in the fictional village of **_Aidensfield_** — centre of much of the action in **Heartbeat.** During the filming of the series the **Goathland**

Hotel is transformed into the **Aidensfield Arms** where the famous **Aidensfield Fire** has burned in the grate for 100 years without ever going out. Directly opposite the hotel is the **Inn On The Moor** which becomes "Base Camp" to the cast and crew of Yorkshire Television. You can follow the waymarked path down the side of the Mallyan Spout Hotel to the dramatic waterfall of that name, or the **Historic Railway Trail** along the route of Stephenson's original railway from the Goathland Hotel.

Goathland

Head out of the village towards Whitby and turn right at the T-junction. Climb steeply up on to the moors and after 2 miles, turn left onto the A169. After ¼ mile turn left

Grosmont Gallery

again towards Grosmont and Egton and drive over Sleights Moor before descending into **Grosmont,** the northern terminus of the North York Moors Railway. Visit the Grosmont Sheds and watch the steam engines being prepared for their daily shift; browse round the **Grosmont Gallery,** a treasure trove of paintings and ceramics by local craftspeople.

Drive down the hill, under the railway bridge and up the steep hill to **Egton.** Bear left part way through the village towards **Egton Bridge** and left again at the T-junction. As you enter the village, turn right by the church towards Glaisdale and left at the junction down Limber Hill. Notice the lovely arched packhorse bridge on the left, Beggar's Bridge, a remnant of Glaisdale's trading days.

Beggar's Bridge

Drive up the hill out of the village and turn right at the junction for **Lealholm.** As you drop down the hill into the village, notice the stepping stones over the River Esk down on the left. Turn left after the bridge towards Danby, passing the **Forge Pottery** and **Shepherd's Hall Tea Rooms,** where fresh home-baked cakes and delicious meals are served throughout the day. Follow the winding minor road along Esk Dale, the largest of the dales within the North York Moors National Park, different from the others in that it runs east to west, not north to south. After 3½ miles you will reach the **Moors Centre,** a countryside interpretation centre complete with brass rubbing facilities and an excellent tea room. Keep left as you head on into Danby village itself, with its high-arched Duck Bridge over the River Esk.

Head over the staggered crossroads to **Castleton** and up the hill on the far side of the village, following signs to Hutton-le-Hole. Climb up along the 1,000-foot high **Castleton Rigg,** with excellent views over Danby Dale to the left, and on over **Blakey Ridge.** Stop off at the lonely **Lion Inn,** at 1,250 feet one of the highest pubs in Yorkshire. A pub since 1553, its busiest times came with the heyday of the Rosedale ironstone mining in the 19th century. Its cosy, low beamed rooms provide an ideal resting place after a hard day's walking over these bleak moors.

Follow the road for a further 6 miles and drop down into the picture postcard village of **Hutton-le-Hole,** with its undulating village green set around Hutton Beck. Call into the **Ryedale Folk Museum,** a record of life in Ryedale through the ages. In the extensive grounds, reconstructed buildings include an Elizabethan manor house, a gypsy caravan and medieval thatched cruck cottage.

Turn right out of the main car park and head up the hill, turning left at the junction to **Lastingham.** This charming but tiny village boasts a long Christian tradition which draws tourists and pilgrims alike. The Lindisfarne monk St. Cedd chose this spot for his monastery which was destroyed by the Danes in A.D. 866 and partially rebuilt in 1078. The original crypt can be entered today through St. Mary's parish church and is used for special services.

Drop down through the village and bear right by the Blacksmiths Arms to **Appleton-le-Moors.** Turn left at the junction, into the village, and, 2 miles further on, turn left onto the A170 and drive through Wrelton to **Aislaby. Aislaby Pottery** is on the right, where you will find original prints and paintings as well as delightful glazed stoneware. Continue through the pretty village of Middleton to Pickering.

DRIVE 2 — (87 miles)
CAPTAIN COOK COUNTRY

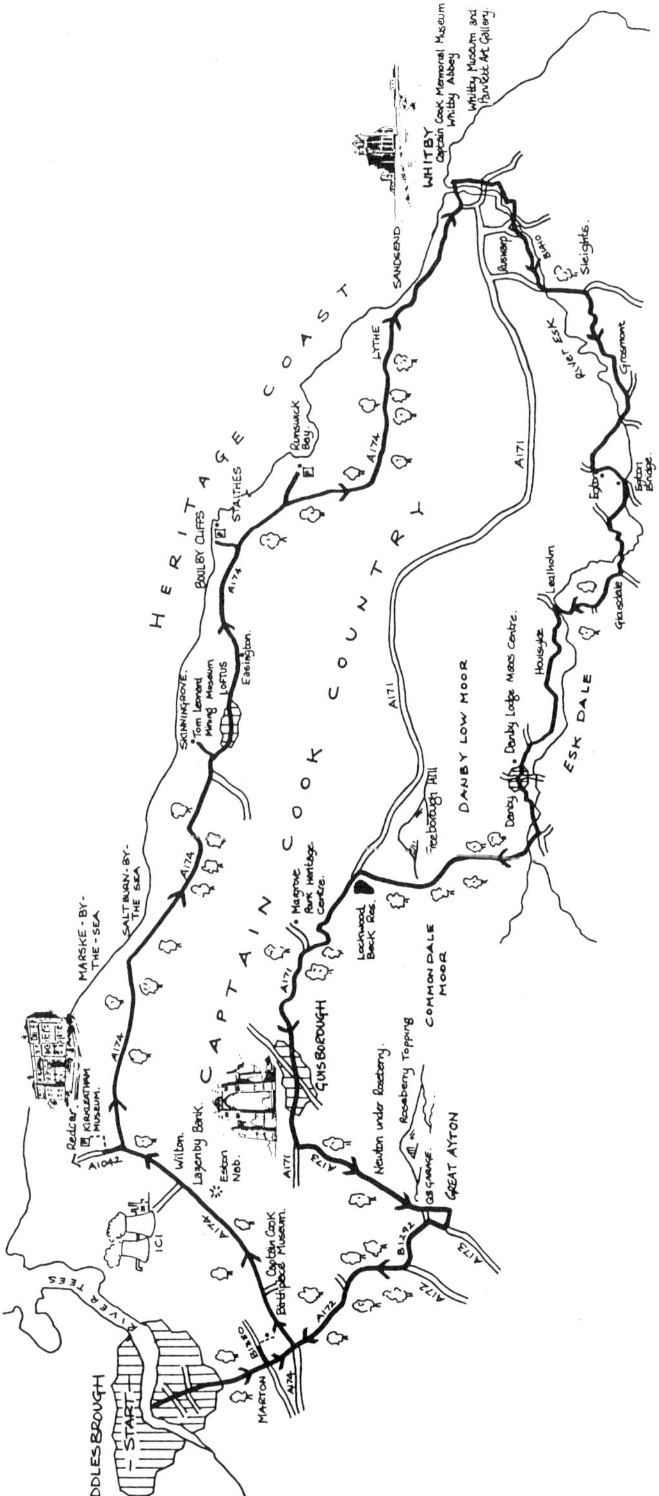

Captain Cook Memorial Museum
Whitby Abbey
Whitby Museum and Pannett Art Gallery

WHITBY

HERITAGE COAST

Runswick Bay

SANDSEND

LYTHE

A174

STAITHES

Ruswarp

Ruswarp

Boxo

River Esk

Grosmont

Sleights

Egton

Egton
Bridge

BOULBY CLIFFS

LOFTUS

Easington

SKINNINGROVE

Tom Leonard
Mining Museum

CAPTAIN   COOK   COUNTRY

A174

A171

ESK DALE

Glaisdale

Lealholm

Houlsyke

Danby · Danby Lodge Moors Centre.

DANBY LOW MOOR

Freebrough Hill

A171

SALTBURN-BY-
THE SEA

MARSKE-BY-
THE-SEA

Redcar ·
KIRKLEATHAM
MUSEUM

A174

Margrove
Park Heritage
Centre

Lockwood
Beck Res.

COMMONDALE
MOOR

A171

GUISBOROUGH

A173

Roseberry Topping

Newton under Roseberry

Gt. Grange

GREAT AYTON

A172

A171

A1042

Wilton.

Lazenby Bank.

Eston
Nab.

A174

A1042

ICI

Captain Cook
Birthplace Museum

MARTON

A174

A172

A172

RIVER   TEES

MIDDLESBROUGH

START

24

This tour explores the area of HEARTBEAT country which is famous for the birth and early career of one of North Yorkshire's most famous sons — Captain James Cook.

Follow the **Captain Cook Heritage Trail** from Middlesbrough down the Heritage Coast to Whitby, through the tranquil dales and villages of Cleveland and North Yorkshire; visit some of the places associated with Cook's early life, and others which preceded him by several centuries.

The tour begins in **Middlesbrough,** an obscure hamlet in James Cook's day, on the south bank of the River Tees. Call into the **Cleveland Centre,** one of Middlesbrough's 3 indoor shopping malls, and see the one fifth scale replica of the H.M.S. Endeavour in which Cook sailed to survey the eastern coast of Australia.

Travel south from Middlesbrough along the A172 Stokesley road, past the South Cleveland Hospital. Look out for the brown and white signs for the **Captain Cook Birthplace Museum.** James Cook would not recognise this as his birthplace of Marton but would surely approve of this fine museum, set in 113 acres of parkland. Displays cover the great explorer's early life in the area, his three great voyages of discovery and the lands he visited. In the Conservatory you'll find species of tropical plants Cook and his botanists would have discovered on their travels. A granite vase behind the conservatory marks the site of the cottage where Cook was born in 1728.

Return to the A172 and drive on towards Stokesley through **Marton** village, past St. Cuthbert's Church on the right, where Cook was baptised. Turn left onto the A174 to Redcar and Saltburn. The Eston Hills are straight ahead, with Eston Nab, an ancient Iron Age fort, clearly visible on the skyline. Bear right at the first roundabout to Redcar, and at the next roundabout, follow the signs for **Kirkleatham Old Hall Museum** on the A1042 Redcar road. This 18th century building, originally a free school, houses many paintings of Cook Country, including work by the "Staithes

Group" of impressionist painters: Laura Knight and Ernest Dade drew their inspiration from the very coastal areas of Cleveland and North Yorkshire that so inspired Captain Cook. Return to the roundabout and continue along the A174 to **Saltburn,** over a series of roundabouts. Set high on a cliff overlooking the sea, Saltburn developed as a Victorian spa town with the coming of the railway in 1861. The golden Victorian era is celebrated here every August with the famous **Victorian Celebrations** — well worth a visit! Descend the steep winding road down to Old Saltburn, past the pier with its water balanced cliff lift and along the sea front past the Ship Inn — frequented by many a smuggler in years gone by. Follow the A174 down the Heritage Coast into **Brotton** and turn left at the T-junction to Whitby. Continue through **Loftus** and **Easington;** soon you will see Boulby Potash mine down to the right which extends miles beneath the sea to reach vast quantities of rock salt, a basic material used in Middlesbrough's chemical industry.

Boulby Cliffs

Over to the left are **Boulby Cliffs,** the highest cliffs on the east coast of England,

Whitby Harbour

riddled with old alum and ironstone levels. A mile or so further on, turn left to **Staithes** and drive to the Old Station car park at the top of a steep hill. Visitors must leave their cars here and walk down into this "olde worlde" fishing village where Cook was apprenticed at the age of 17. The sea-front haberdashers shop where Cook worked has long since gone, swallowed up by the sea, but the rebuilt shop stands near the harbour with its commemorative plaque. Watch the cobles unload their catch of lobster and look out for the women wearing the traditional "Staithes bonnets", once a very familiar sight!

Staithes

Return to the A174 and after approximately 2 miles turn left down a steep hill to **Runswick Bay** car park. Wander along the twisting footpaths between the red-roofed cottages and miniature gardens and enjoy magnificent views over the bay.

Return to the A174 and drive on to Whitby through **Lythe.** As you head down Lythe Bank, take in the spectacular views over the bay at Sandsend. Pass through

Sandsend and continue into the bustling old seaport of **Whitby (*"Strensford"?*)** at the mouth of the River Esk, following the signs for the town centre. As you drop down the hill past Pannet Park on the right, follow the one-way system down Brunswick Street to the harbour area car park. Here, Cook learned the trade of mariner and you can visit the charming 18th century harbourside house in Grape Lane where he lodged whilst working for Walker, the Whitby shipowner, now the **Captain Cook Memorial Museum.** Wander round the Old Town with its smugglers' yards, tea rooms and craft shops; climb the 199 steps up to **Whitby Abbey** and **St. Mary's Church;** relive some of the scenes from Bram Stoker's novel "Dracula" at the award-winning **Dracula Experience Museum —** not for the faint-hearted!

Drive over the swing bridge across the estuary, (signposted "the Abbey") and continue to the staggered crossroads at the top of the hill. Go straight across up Larpool Lane, past the Larpool Hall Hotel and down through the woods to a T-junction. Turn right over a metal bridge and immediately left to Sleights and Pickering, to drive along the River Esk. Drive on to a T-junction and turn left over Sleights Bridge into the village. Turn right on the far side to Grosmont and the North York Moors Railway and follow the winding country road with magnificent views over Esk Dale on the right. Descend the hill into **Grosmont,** the northern terminus of the North York Moors Railway. A visit to the Grosmont sheds is a must for any steam engine enthusiast to see the beautiful engines being prepared for their daily shift. Browse around the **Grosmont Gallery** which houses the works of local potters and painters, and call into the Hazelwood Tea Rooms next door for a tempting selection of home-made cakes and scones to help you on your way. Drive down the hill, under the railway bridge and on into **Egton.** Bear left as you enter the village towards **Egton Bridge** and left again down a steep bank into the village. You will find a free car park on the right just before the church.

Turn right out of the car park and immediately right to Glaisdale, along a very pretty stretch of the Esk. Turn left at the junction and continue down Limber Hill into peaceful **Glaisdale.** Notice the lovely stone arched Beggar's Bridge on the left. Head up the hill out of the village and turn right at the T-junction to **Lealholm.** Drive down past the Stepping Stones antiquarian book shop on the left, named after the nearby stepping stones across the river Esk. Go over the bridge and turn left to Danby. Stop off at **Poet's Cottage Nursery;** take home a memento from the pottery housed in the old forge; call into **Shepherd's Hall Tea Rooms,** the former meeting place of The Loyal Order of Ancient Shepherds Friendly Society and tuck into a delicious cream tea or succulent ham and eggs!

Follow the twisting minor road along the Esk valley, through Houlsyke and on to **The Moors Visitor Centre** at Danby Lodge with its interpretive displays of rural life, nature trails and brass rubbing facilities. Drive on into **Danby** village and head straight on at the staggered crossroads to **Castleton.** Turn right part way through the village to Guisborough and head over the moors to meet the A171 by Lockwood Beck.

Turn left and after 4½ miles you will enter **Guisborough,** the ancient Capital of Cleveland with its ruined **Augustinian Priory** founded by Robert de Brus. The cobbled high street hosts a wonderful market on Thursdays and Saturdays. Leave the town on the A171 Teesside road and at the second roundabout, turn left onto the A173. The distinctive anvil-shaped profile of Roseberry Topping looms up ahead, "Cleveland's Matterhorn"!

Drive on through Newton-under-Roseberry towards **Great Ayton** and turn left by the Q8 garage, following the signs for the Captain Cook Schoolroom Museum. This delightful village on the banks of the River Leven was Cook's childhood home. Visit the 12th century **All Saints' Church** where his mother and 5 of his brothers and sisters are buried; the **Captain Cook Monument** can be seen in the distance high up on Easby Moor. Just beyond the village green is **Suggitts,** whose delicious ice cream is well known throughout the area. Nearby, the **Schoolroom Museum** occupies part of the building where Cook was educated: learn all about Cook and his voyages and 18th century Great Ayton as Cook would have known it.

Drive on to the bridge and turn right up Guisborough road before turning left onto the B1292 to Middlesbrough. Turn right at the crossroads and follow the A172 back to your starting point.

DRIVE 3 — (70 miles)
THE CLEVELAND AND HAMBLETON HILLS

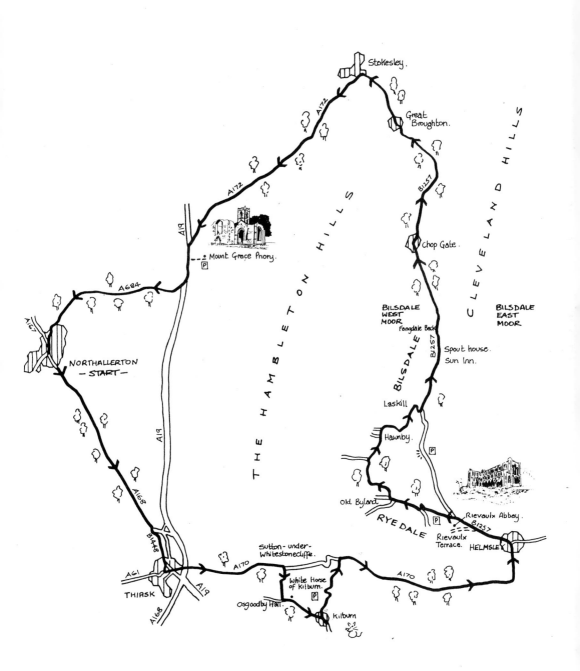

Stokesley.

Great Broughton.

A172

A172

A19

Mount Grace Priory.

A684

A167

NORTHALLERTON
— START —

A19

Chop Gate

B1257

THE HAMBLETON HILLS

CLEVELAND HILLS

BILSDALE
WEST
MOOR

Fangdale Beck

BILSDALE
EAST
MOOR

B1257

BILSDALE

Spout house.
Sun Inn.

Laskill

Hawnby.

A168

Old Byland.

Rievaulx Abbey.

RYEDALE

B1257

Rievaulx Terrace.

HELMSLEY

B1448

A61

THIRSK

A19

A168

Sutton - under -
Whitestonecliffe.

A170

White Horse
of Kilburn.

A170

Osgoodby Hall.

Kilburn

The drive begins in the centre of **Northallerton,** County Town of North Yorkshire, with its elegant red brick buildings and broad High Street. Browse round the quality shops and boutiques in Barkers Arcade, or step back in time in Lewis and Cooper's renowned delicatessen. **Betty's Cafe and Bakery** is now a national institution and serves mouth-watering breads and cakes made from a unique combination of Yorkshire and Swiss recipes.

Follow the signs for Thirsk, leaving Northallerton by the A168. Continue for 7 miles, then turn right onto the B1448. Drive into **Thirsk,** a traditional Yorkshire market town with its cobbled streets and old coaching inns, full of interesting nooks and crannies. Described by James Herriot as a "happy town", Thirsk is home to the real-life Herriot veterinary practice situated in Kirkgate. Visit **Thirsk Folk Museum,** housed in the birthplace of Thomas Lord, founder of Lord's cricket ground, where Herriot's original manuscripts are displayed. From the town centre, take the A170 towards Scarborough. As you drop down into the village of **Sutton-under-Whitestonecliffe,** look out for **Colin Almack's** studio, at the sign of the beaver: here you can acquire anything from cupboards and chairs to bread boards and book-ends, all beautifully fashioned from English oak and sporting the distinctive carved beaver.

You are now heading for the "heart" of HEARTBEAT COUNTRY. Continue towards Scarborough on the A170 and take the first right turn towards Kilburn. Follow the narrow country road to a T-junction by the elegant Jacobean manor house Osgoodby Hall. Turn left here and right at the bottom of the hill into **Kilburn,** and park in the square by the Forester's Arms Hotel. Famous as the home of "Mouseman Thompson", the renowned carved mouse is still found on every piece of furniture produced by **Robert Thompson's Craftsmen** whose studio is based in Thompson's old home, a half-timbered house

in the main street. Across the road, Thompson's original workshop and adjoining blacksmiths shop house a new visitor centre where you can watch craftsmen at work and fascinating videos. You will find further examples of Thompson's work in the little church off the central square.

Robert Thompson's Studio

Turn right out of the village square and follow the winding road towards Sutton Bank. Take the first left turn for White Horse Bank and climb the steep 1:4 gradient (not for the faint hearted driver!) towards the **White Horse of Kilburn** on the hillside ahead. After ½ mile turn left into the Forestry Commission car park just below the horse. 314 feet long and 228 feet high, the turf-cut figure was designed by John Hodgson, headmaster of the village school, and completed with the help of his pupils and local volunteers using gallons of whitewash!

Turn left out of the car park and continue up the steep narrow road, past the Yorkshire Gliding Club and on to the junction with the A170. Turn right and continue on to the ancient stone market town of **Helmsley,** with its spacious market square and 12th century castle. Visit **Duncombe Park,** the ancestral home of Lord Feversham, an elegant 18th century baroque mansion set in 300 acres of dramatic parkland around the River Rye, with classical temples, tree-lined terraces and the tallest ash and lime trees in England!

From Helmsley, follow the B1257 Stokesley road for 2 miles and take a left turn into the driveway of **Rievaulx Terrace and Temples,** formerly part of the Duncombe estate, now owned by the National Trust. The grassy walk, bounded at each end by a classical temple, once made a perfect setting for elaborate family picnic parties. Visit the Ionic Temple, set out for a banquet, and the exhibition on the Duncombe family.

Turn sharp left out of the drive down Rievaulx Bank and drive on past delightful thatched cottages to **Rievaulx Abbey** car park. The well-preserved ruins of this Cistercian abbey date from 1132, an impressive sight cradled amongst the wooded hills.

Turn left out of the car park and right at the junction over Rievaulx bridge towards Scawton and Old Byland. Watch out for a right turn to Cold Kirby and Old Byland and pass over a narrow bridge and up the hill through Ashberry Woods.

As you enter Old Byland, bear right down a narrow lane towards Hawnby. Turn right at the T-junction and then right again. Continue down the steep hill and bear left at the junction. Drive on through the village and as you approach the top of the hill on the far side, turn right for Laskill. The narrow, winding road leads on over a little bridge up a steep bank with wonderful views over Bilsdale West Moor to the left and Rievaulx Moor ahead. Drive over the narrow bridge into **Laskill** and follow the road round to the left, turning left at the junction onto the B1257. Head on up Bilsdale and after 2 miles, look out for the Sun Inn, a square stone building on the

right. Adjacent is **Spout House,** a 16th century cruck-framed thatched cottage. Originally a farm tenant's cottage, it later served as a farmhouse and an ale house, the Sun Inn, before the new, larger inn was built across the yard. Now open to the public again, the character of the building has changed little since that day when last orders were called for the last time!

Continue along the B1257, passing through Chop Gate and Great Broughton before driving on into **Stokesley.** This gracious little town on the banks of the River Leven is bustling with activity on Fridays, market day. Explore the narrow alleys which lead off Main Street to the grassy banks of the river with its little bridges and ducks; admire the fine Georgian and Regency buildings that line the High Street.

Follow the signs for the A172 (Thirsk) and after 7 miles fork left for Thirsk. The road merges with the A19 (South); take the first turning left, following the white on brown signs for **Mount Grace Priory,** the best preserved Carthusian monastery in the country. Here you can see the monks' cells, church, stables and brew house, while the Priory Guest House contains a history of the order.

Return to the A19 (South) and after just over ½ mile, bear left along the A684 back to Northallerton.

Having seen the splendour of the North York Moors for yourself, it is easy to understand how Peter Walker, then a young country "bobby", became inspired to write about his life and times in this area during the 1960's. Despite the march of time and progress, little has changed in 30 years.

ACKNOWLEDGEMENTS

C.P. Printing and Publishing Ltd. and Ashley and Newey Ltd. wish to thank the many individuals and organisations who have helped to make this book possible. In particular, thanks must go to the staff and crew of Yorkshire Television, and the actors themselves, for their patience and co-operation.

Acknowledgement is due to the following individuals for permission to reproduce photographs:-

Yorkshire Television	9.
Geordie Stephenson	1, 2, 3, 4, 5, 6, 7, 19, 21 (right), 22, 25, 26, 27, 30.
Ben Smith	12, 14 (top), 15 (top), 18, 22 (right).
North York Moors Railway	21 (left).
Nigel Allison	8, 10, 11, 14 (bottom), 15 (bottom).

Front Cover by Nigel Allison.

Maps and illustrations by Steve Darke.

This publication has been designed and produced by C.P. Offset Ltd., Darlington's finest printers.

Written by Ben Smith
Edited by Caroline Alderson.

ISBN 1 873293 53 4.

Second Edition 1994.